Mixed Nuts

Written by Mai-Lis F. Bahr
Illustrated by Katerinka Kirik

Text copyright ©2019
Illustrations Copyright ©2019
First Edition 2019
Published by People of Charlotte CLT, LLC
All rights reserved.

No part of this book may be reproduced or transmitted in any form or by any means, electronic or mechanical, including photocopying, recording, or by any information storage and retrieval system, without permission in writing from the author.

This book is a work of fiction. Any similarity between the characters and situations; within its pages, places or persons, living or dead; is unintentional and coincidental.

Library of Congress
Control Number: 2019930520

All inquiries should be addressed to:
peopleofCLT@gmail.com

ISBN: 978-0-9985615-1-6

10 9 8 7 6 5 4 3 2 1

Thank you, Carson and Addie, for continually turning me towards all the positivity in the world. And thank you, Chris, for always encouraging me in all that I do.

This book belongs to:

Everyone

Peanut Place was a very nice place to live. Mr. and Mrs. Peanut lived there with all their friends and family. The Peanuts had their own way of singing songs and playing games. To them, everything was just right.

One day, Mr. and Mrs. Walnut came into town and needed a place to live. They saw the Peanuts of Peanut Place looked happy, so they wanted to live there too.

Mr. and Mrs. Walnut asked the Peanuts, "May we live at Peanut Place?"

The Peanuts of Peanut Place replied, "No, you are Walnuts and not like us. Walnuts do not know how to sing songs and play games the Peanut way."

Mr. and Mrs. Walnut were quite sad.

They needed a happy place to live, and they thought Peanut Place would be just right.

Mr. Walnut said to Mrs. Walnut, "We can find another place to live. Maybe there will be some Walnuts somewhere in town." Together they began walking down the street with their suitcases.

While out for a walk, Mr. and Mrs. Peanut saw the sad and lonely Walnuts.

Mr. and Mrs. Peanut agreed that perhaps they were not as friendly as they should have been to the Walnuts. Together, Mr. and Mrs. Peanut invited the Walnuts to stay with them.

Mr. and Mrs. Walnut were so happy to have a place that they could call home at Peanut Place. Some of the Peanuts heard about their new neighbors and did not like the news.

They still thought the Walnuts were too different and would never do things the Peanut way.

One day, Salty and Honey Peanut could not believe their ears! They heard the most beautiful sound coming out of Mr. and Mrs. Peanut's home.

Salty and Honey had never heard Peanuts sing songs that way before. They rushed over to the Peanut's home to hear more.

To their surprise, Mr. and Mrs. Walnut answered the door. Salty Peanut asked, "Who was singing that beautiful song?" Mr. Walnut answered, "Why? It was us. Did you really like it?"

Honey Peanut replied, "Oh yes! It was magical! We have never sung that way before!"

For the rest of the afternoon, Mr. and Mrs. Walnut, Salty, and Honey sang many songs the Walnut way.

All of Peanut Place soon heard their happy voices and joined in. For the first time, Peanut Place echoed with a new sound.

The Peanuts asked the Walnuts to invite their friends and family to live at Peanut Place. Soon Peanut Place became a home to many different kinds of nuts.

They all welcomed the Pecans, the Cashews, the Almonds, and the Brazils.

Peanut Place was no longer just a place for Peanuts. It was now a place for all kinds of nuts.

The Peanut Place sign just wasn't right anymore, so all the nuts agreed on a new name: Mixed Nuts Place!

Mixed Nuts Place became an even happier and livelier place with so much diversity. The nut families learned from one another and grew to accept new ways of singing, playing, and dancing. The news traveled quickly and many more mixed communities started coming together.

Mr. and Mrs. Peanut smiled at each other as they saw how opening their doors to new neighbors made their community richer and stronger.

The End

Discussion Section

What is diversity?

Diversity: The state of having people who are different races or who have different cultures, in a group or organization.

Now let's use the word "diversity" in a sentence:

1. "The school aims for diversity in its student population."

2. "The city is known for its cultural diversity."

Source: Merriam-Webster's Learner's Dictionary

How are we similar?

We all have feelings and want to be loved and respected. We wish to be included among groups of people and to have friends. We all have skin, hair, ears, a nose, eyes, arms, and legs.

Sometimes we play the same sports or participate in the same activities. Sometimes we also celebrate the same holidays.

How are we different?

Our hair color and texture, eye color, skin color, freckles, and body shapes and sizes can be different. Languages, religions, cultural traditions, and beliefs may differ. Hobbies, jobs, interests, and talents can differ as well.

Let's explore diversity some more:

Diversity means there are different types, a variety. There are different kinds and colors of toys, cars, trains, and other objects that you see every day. You also see people with differences every day. Wouldn't it be boring if every car was exactly the same in color, shape, and size? Well, the same applies to our friends, neighbors, and other people in the world. Our world would not be very interesting if we were all the same. Our differences make us unique and interesting, allowing us to contribute in many different ways.

Diversity can also be found in our own homes. Moms and dads can be of different races, siblings can have different hair color, and all family members can like different activities. Diversity can be found in schools, workplaces, shopping centers, and other public places.

What's great about diversity?

Diversity introduces us to other ways of living. When we share the music, food, clothing, and traditions that we like, we share our diversity. When we learn about one another and learn to enjoy what others enjoy, we become less scared of change. We become open to different ways of living, different appearances, and likes.

What can be challenging about diversity?

Diversity can cause fear and misunderstandings. We may not allow someone to participate in an activity just because they are different.

We may show unkindness by deciding not to like someone before getting to know them. Unkindness can be shown by not allowing someone to participate in an activity based on their gender. When someone is treated unfairly like this, it is called discrimination.

How can you grow from diversity?

Next time, when you see someone who is different from you, think about how much you can learn from them.

Also, think about how their differences and your differences both make your worlds more interesting.

Mai-Lis Bahr is a resident of Charlotte, NC, where she resides with her husband, two children, and two dogs. While growing up in Saratoga Springs, NY, Mai-Lis used her imagination to take her places, as well as dream about the future, which she still does to this day. While tutoring for the Augustine Literacy Project, Mai-Lis met a little boy with whom she shared many conversations about diversity, inspiring *Mixed Nuts*. Currently, Mai-Lis is working on a novel, as well as publishing real stories on her website, PeopleofCLT.com.

Made in the USA
Middletown, DE
02 March 2023